Acknowledgement & Dedication

The man on the front cover is my Dad. The picture was taken probably before I was born – before I was ever conceived.

Thanks, Dad. You taught me so much about gardening, farming, sowing seed and harvesting that it has made studying the Bible so much easier.

Lots of Love!

Do Not Orphan Your Seed

All Scripture references are from KJV unless otherwise indicated.

Freshwater Press, USA

ISBN# 998-8-9868502—8-3

Copyright 2022 by Dr. Marlene Miles

All rights reserved. No part of this book may be reproduced, distributed, or transmitted by any means or in any means including photocopying, recording or other electronic or mechanical methods without prior written permission of the publisher except in the case of brief publications or critical reviews.

This book is part of **The Fold** series. The purpose of that series is to answer the question: Why some 30, some 60, and some-100-fold return in the Offering.

The Fold series of books follows **Power Money: Nine Times the Tithe** which puts forth that the tithe must be paid first before any offering anointing will work. It discusses in revelatory detail---, *why*. Two other books in the series are **Name Your Seed**, and the **Poor Attitudes of Money**.

Table of Contents

Abandoned Seed 6
Substance of Faith 13
Prayer for Salvation and Seed Prosperity 16
A Sowing Journal 18
Nomads Don't Farm 26
Put Your Money Where Your Mouth Is 28
Orphaned Seed 33
The *spirit* Matters 36
Prayer for Abandoned Seeds 39
Multiple *Partners*, Multiple Altars 42
Broken Hearts 47
Prayer: Breaking Soul Ties 52
About the Author 55
Books by this author 56

Do Not

Orphan Your Seeds

Freshwater Press

USA

Abandoned Seed

Always **parent** your seed--, every seed, and every kind of seed.

Husbandry is stewardship and we are called to be wise stewards over the works of God's hands. We have all kinds of seeds in our possession and around us all day, every day. Natural seeds that are or will become our children. Natural seeds that become plants, flowers, trees. And spiritual seeds which is how we speak of money sown in the Offerings at our churches, for example. In spiritual sowing, God says we can expect 30, 60, and 100-fold return in our giving.

This book is an addendum to the first two books of **The Fold,** *Receiving 30, 60, and 100-fold Returns, Name Your Seed is the next book.* The last book is, **The Poor Attitudes of Money.** There is so much more in those books, get them if you don't already have them.

Warning: Do not *orphan* your seeds if you want to realize 30, 60 and 100-fold return in Offerings.

Ever see a farmer standing in the middle of a field with nothing in it? Ever see a farmer go back to a field with <u>nothing</u> in it, *daily*? If you're a city dweller, or you've never noticed a farmer doing this, then you've never seen a farmer doing what he really does. His going out to the "empty" fields, is the *substance* of what he hopes for.

That is Faith.

The farmer is growing crops from seeds to harvest to feed his family, his community, or to sell at market to make a profit to take care of his obligations. Our farmer has a vested interest in his crop coming up and reaching harvest. Even if he is a perfect financial steward with good savings, he *needs* this crop; he needs his seeds to perform. Else, it's just wasted seeds. Else it's just wasted time, having sown seeds, and cultivating them but seeing no or little return is not profitable and it's not God's way. The seeds he sows have to perform. They have to harvest to create abundance.

I plant gardens around my home. My gardens are diagrammed. I know what plant, what bulb, what flower, seeds, and bushes are *where*. I know what is expected next season and next year and what is not. I know what I have to replant in what season. I know what is annual, and what is perennial.

I'm a gardener. If I were a farmer, I'd know what field my corn was in, and in what field my wheat is planted, and so on. I'd know approximately what day which seed should come up, bloom, bear fruit, and harvest. I'd check on it daily. I'd go back to the field even before the seed came up, knowing and having full expectancy that the seed *would* come up. I'd have a good idea of when. This is why farmers stay home in the growing and harvesting seasons--, **expectancy**, and that's a part of faith.

Nomads and wanderers don't plant seeds; they don't garden.

Don't you hang around to check on your crops, that is your bank accounts, investments, or have access to doing so even when you travel? A farmer can't check on his fields on vacation. That's why he's home most of the year--, or all year, really.

Ever see a pregnant woman who doesn't look pregnant take prenatal vitamins? That's Faith. That's Wisdom. That's the **substance** of what she hopes for. Even in the first trimester, before she begins to show, she checks her figure daily, as does the farmer, he checks on his planted, but as of yet, ungrown field. At first it doesn't look like anything is in there, but they both know there is.

Maybe you need to diagram your spiritual sowing. Since some of your planted spiritual seed hasn't come up or some may be delayed in coming up, you may need to journal your sowing. I'd refer to this as a **sowing journal**. Like gardens, farmers, and pregnant women, you've got to know what you sowed, when you sowed it and what is supposed to come up, and *when*.

As you are not a wanderer, you actually live somewhere, you sow where you **LIVE**. If you sow elsewhere, *with permission*, you've got to come back to see about your seed. Many people don't come back to check on what they sowed, not daily--, not ever. They just sow it and wait for a miracle.

Many fields are *not* empty, but no one came back to check on the growth or harvest; they left off working that field. Those fields are *unclaimed*. If you're going to get your harvest by a miracle, you wouldn't need to sow, you could just wait for the miracle. Sowing is explained to us in the Bible, although parts of how it grows and reaches maturity is a mystery.

The multiplication of any sowing is because of God--, whether a natural seed growing into a baby to birth, or a spiritual, financial seed multiplying to 30, 60 and 100-fold returns. The abundant harvest is expected, but it can still be miraculous.

And he said, So is the kingdom of God, as if a man should cast seed into the ground;

And should sleep, and rise night and day, and the seed should spring and grow up, he knoweth not how.

For the earth bringeth forth fruit of herself; first the blade, then the ear, after that the full corn in the ear.

But when the fruit is brought forth, immediately he putteth in the sickle, because the harvest is come. Matthew 4:26-29

Substance of Faith

As further *substance* of faith, we discuss **naming** your seed in **Book 2** of **The Fold** series, entitled, **Name Your Seed**. But if you're going to discuss *seed* with God, He will need to know *what seed* you're talking about, which is one of the reasons you should **name your seed**.

Faith has *substance*. **Naming your seed** is *substance*.

Would you have a baby and not *name* it? This seed you have sown that God has received lives. *Name it.*

When you're talking to God about your natural children, do you call them by name, or do you just refer to them as your *seed*?

Regarding care and nurture, leaving your seed in unskilled, uncaring, unwise, or unspiritual hands is not prudent either. When you leave your children home with other children, they don't always take care of your little ones as you'd like them to. Yet you may do this every time you leave your children home alone to go to your *second* job. Your older children (seeds) may be completely negligent, for all you know. Don't leave seed to chase after or watch over seed. Seed is too young, unwise, and inexperienced to watch seed. No wonder your seeds don't seem to be prospering.

It's also what you do when you sow offering seed, forgetting it, orphaning it, and sowing a new one. Do the better thing, watch over your seed, it's more precious and worth more than a few dollars from a second job. The harvest you'd receive from properly ministering to your **main seed** far outweighs what you could get from improperly ministering to more than one seed, both natural and financial.

If you have made a habit of abandoning seed, why would God *receive* your most recent seed sown? Repent. Do it today.

Prayer for Salvation and Seed Prosperity

Father, by the work of Jesus at Calvary I am redeemed from the Curse of the Law. I believe in my heart and have confessed that Jesus is Your Son. He died and on the third day You resurrected Him. Thank You, Lord.

As I am called to be a wise steward in the Earth, Father I repent and ask forgiveness for poor stewardship over any areas of my life: Relationships, Finances, Education, Career, Profession, Marriage, Family, home--, everything you've put under my watch. Lord, cover it all with the Blood of Jesus.

I repent for poor management and handling in the sowing of financial seed. I repent of not tithing and will purpose to be a faithful tither. I repent of distractions and being drawn away from Kingdom work by the lusts of this world.

Thank You, Father for access into the 30, 60, and 100-Fold of returns in Offerings. I repent of having sown seeds in doubt, unbelief, under duress, under peer pressure and then just walking away, NOT BELIEVING that You would return to me some 30, or 60, or 100-Fold of what I offered sincerely to You.

Lord, redeem the time, resurrect any and all seed that can be resurrected, grown, and matured and harvested that I will have all things that pertain to life and to godliness and that You will be glorified.

I praise and honor You Lord, I know that Your Word is true because you are not a man that You should lie. Lord, help my unbelief and show me how to minister to my sown seeds that the harvest will be plenteous, abundant, even more than enough, in the matchless Name of Jesus Christ, Amen.

A Sowing Journal

A Sowing Journal is useful to remind yourself of what you've sown for and for what you have *expectancy*. It is not to batter God, or your pastor about how much you've given, and it's not for bragging rights. Yes, count your seed as dead, that is, do not repent of having sown it, but don't forget it. You would never forget that you were having a baby. But why is it so easy for the saints, who are living by faith, to forget they have *seed* in the ground? Faith is **substance** of what you hope for, and what you've sown for. As a little baby or small child, your seed needs ministering to.

You will only minister to your spiritual seed if you **remember** it.

Surprise children?

It could happen, and it's been known to happen. The crops that come up on a farmer's land will never surprise him, not even a weed, although it's not a valued crop. I'm a gardener. Trust me, a pink lily is not going to come up with my white garden unless I plant the seed or bulb there. (Absent of shenanigans.) You won't get something **good** that you didn't sow for outside of the Love, Mercy, and Grace of God.

(Getting something bad that you didn't sow for is not in the scope of this book, but it is very possible. Getting something evil that you **did** sow for – a harvest that you're ashamed of is also the scope of another volume.)

When you don't steward, that is when you are not a *husbandman* to your seed, you **abandon** it, as if the offering was a slot machine and you are just going to put in another quarter or a dollar next Sunday. My point is if your Offering is so small that you will not even miss it – you will not give it another thought. Five dollars? One dollar?

Or, if you sow with weak faith, if you don't believe that anything is going to come of what you sowed anyway, why would you give it another thought? These are unprofitable attitudes about sowing and money.

What about what you already sowed? You steward over what you have, what you are going to have, and you have responsibility to what you're *supposed to* have. You have to guard what you have, keep it from being taken or stolen from you and also to INCREASE. You increase the Kingdom by increasing your own financial standing in the Earth. This is not arrogance, this is kingship. Little "k" kings are supposed to be increasing their domain.

If you don't have enough faith to **remember** that you sowed a seed, write it down. Write the vision. The vision is a field full of mature corn with golden tassels sparkling in the sunshine. The vision is enough money to pay off your mortgage completely. The vision is more than enough to send your children, debt-free to college. What is the vision? Write it in your sowing journal. Make it plain. Talk to God about it DAILY.

Until it manifests.

Then Praise God some more. Tithe. Be a blessing and sow, some more!!! Prove God. He loves to be proved!!!

In baking, "proving" is what we Americans call rising. Yeast is put in bread, and some time goes by while the bread dough is in a certain environment (temperature). The bread dough rises, sometimes doubling or tripling in size. Then it's ready to be baked. The proving makes it fluffy, airy, yummy. Prove GOD, watch Him MULTIPLY your seed to harvest. Watch Him enlarge your tent. Watch God turn a simple seed in to a 30, 60 or 100-fold harvest.

Enter *In*

You are to daily enter into the Courts where you have seed planted, even if the Field of that Court is empty. Habakkuk says, *Even though the barns are empty, I will yet praise Him.* This is how you **minister to your seed and to your Field.** Enter into praise, at least daily, but more often is better saying, *Lord, thank You for Your wonderful mercies toward me. You deserve praise; You are worthy. I praise You for the anointing on this seed in this Field, which is anointed to prosper seed. I thank You for allowing me to sow and abide in Your Fold, in Your Courts.*

I thank You for this planted seed. I see a healthy field of blessings, corresponding to the seed I have sown. I've named the seed _____ (whatever you've named it), *and I expect and see* (spiritually*) a field of* _____*growing, blooming, bearing fruit, and coming to fullness. I thank You, Lord, for perfecting the seed and all that concerns me. I thank You and praise You for all of the works of Your hand and for blessing the seed, and in all that I set my hands to do. I worship You in the beauty of holiness, and since all these things reproduce after their kind, so does my seed.*

I declare all things in Heaven and Earth obey the Word of the Lord, and so my Field is full, and overflowing with the harvest of blessings. I determine to check on my Field often--, at least daily, staying the required time to see this seed to full harvest, that I may reap 100-fold to the praise of Your Glory, in Jesus Name, Amen.

All that is said while standing in what looks like an empty field. All that, Monday morning regarding the seed you just sowed Sunday afternoon, even if you see nothing, not one plant, not even a weed. Now we're talking about some Faith--, and that's real **substance**. No one is going to get a 30, 60, or preferably a 100-fold harvest without some real Faith.

When a man and woman are expecting a child, even before the tummy gets rounded, they still know that they are expecting, and they don't forget it. If you sowed with expectancy, and it was *received* by God--, Congratulations! It's a son and you should have full expectancy. Under normal circumstances, no sane parent would let a doctor take their baby at 30-fold (3 months) and not at 60-fold (6 months). You have full expectancy, intend to wait, pray, and plan for your child and you will hold out for the full 40 weeks, (100%).

That spiritual seed—(it's a son), and you also must have *full expectancy* until you realize full harvest, tangibly. Naturally ministering to your seed means diet, prenatal vitamins, Lamaze, doctor's visits, moderate exercise, the whole 9 yards, (9 months, as we say). *Spiritually*, that means taking in the Word, worship, praise, assembling yourself in the church, prayer, spiritual warfare, counseling, whatever is necessary to get yourself in shape to give birth to a happy, healthy *harvest* from your sown, *received, and n*urtured seed.

Don't orphan your seed.

Nomads Don't Farm

There is a growing season for every crop. The reason some may only experience 30-fold return is because they tend to their crop only 30% of what is necessary, 30% of what is needed. Ministering to your seed not even half the way, diminishes returns.

Nomads don't garden at all. If you're wandering from pillar to post, from camp to camp, from church to church, from *fold* to *fold*, and within that from Court to Court, what do you expect to receive from the Lord? If you don't spend enough time in the Court (place where you sowed the seed) your seed will not have enough ministry and *time* to reach maturity and to reach its full harvest. Don't sow and then leave the Field and the seed, spiritually speaking.

If you are a nomad--, a spiritual nomad, why even sow a spiritual seed? Why?

Some harvests can be taken early and just reduced in size. These are probably the 30, or 60-fold returns. They're considered premature because God loves fullness and wholeness. When taking fields early, they do not yield what they could. (This correlates in the banking world, *Substantial penalty for early withdrawal.*) However, taking some harvests early, would mean **no harvest at all**.

Put Your Money Where Your Mouth Is

You sow in the Inner Court because that's where you *LIVE*. You **LIVE** there. After you've sown, you go to the *Field* of the Inner Court, even when that Field appears empty, to check on what you sowed. You go <u>daily</u> until the growth starts. You go while the seed is growing. And you go until full harvest manifests. Even when it looks like what you prayed and sowed for isn't happening, you keep going to check on it anyway. Keep believing that it will and has come to pass and that is how you use faith, and what you use faith for.

If you sowed in the Inner Court but never come back to the Inner Court, instead get slack or discouraged only coming to Thanksgiving--, your **Field** is not there. What must you do? Did you put your money where your mouth is? Did you sow your seed where your worship *is*?

In my example of Thanksgiving, Praise and Worship correlate to the Outer Court, the Inner Court and the Holy of Holies, the Inner Court correlates to the *Praise Court*. You've got to press your way into praise **every day** to "check on your Field."

You eat three times a day, don't you? If your intention toward your seed is to grow it, then go *feed* it. Go to your Field at least three times a **day.** Go into the Courts of the Lord at least three times a day. In its growing season if you go 30% of what is needed, you may yield a 30-fold increase. If you go 60%, a 60-fold and so on, depending on many other criteria that you are learning about in this book.

You got to know the *season* of your sowing and reaping. Since you're sowing spiritual seed, the *seasons* are spiritually discerned. Ask God. While you are in Thanksgiving, Praise and Worship, that is a great time to talk to Him about your seeds that you've already sown and **named**. And also talk to Him about seeds that you are planning to sow. God often tells people when, where and what to sow and for what purpose.

You may have just become keenly aware of all the seed that you may have *abandoned* or *orphaned*. The enemy is especially busy, distracting folk to leave off tending their seed. The enemy may set a financial fire as soon as you sow your seed, causing you to repent of ever having sown. As soon as you sowed a respectable seed in the Offering, the washing machine broke. Oh my! You place "blame" on the seed and regret sowing it. You may become angry or vow not to sow again. OK, the enemy wrestled that blessing out of your hand and future without ever wrestling you.

Or the enemy may set an emotional fire to distract you from going to your "Field" to minister to your seed. Instead of going into Praise and Worship, which will minister to your sown seed, you ignore God for a few days in any number of predictable ways. You could spend four days mad at your spouse, two days agonizing, or worrying about your kid, or a week depressed, about your weight, completely forgetting you even planted that seed because by that time, it's Sunday again and you're planting a new one, a new seed.

How about your other son or *sons*? Your seed? How about *those* seeds? Forgotten?

Be of good cheer, be happy if God is allowing you to learn this now, it's because He has good purpose in this teaching and plans of success for you. It is so you don't continue to lose seed due to ignorance, deception, and distraction. It may be that you can repent of the mistakes in your sowing and regain the *time* that you need to minister to your previously sown seed.

Orphaned Seed

Birds--, wild birds, especially, love seeds. The enemies of God always come for the seed.

When you don't properly minister to your seed in the natural, here come the predators. Tiny ones, big ones, visible ones, and invisible ones. They are all potential destroyers of seeds. Are you watching your sown seeds? Your seedlings? Your crops? When you don't minister to financial seeds, in the spiritual is as though you *orphan* it, and it will not prosper to harvest.

The enemies of God are the enemies of SEED, whether that seed is sown or still in the barn. When the seed is sown, it attracts the wild birds. Here they come, in a feeding frenzy. If they can eat up all your seed, they will.

If you've sown seed, you've got to hang around and tend to it. I am not saying don't ever take a break or go on vacation, but don't just toss seed to the ground and forget about it. This kind of behavior is rather brazen and is not profitable.

Maybe you sowed it, but it is bound, stuck in that place between out of your hand and becoming a seedling or a mature harvest. If you haven't ministered to it, then it is dormant. If God is merciful and gracious toward you, you might realize a harvest. If not, what you sowed could be dead if He just let the natural consequences of your negligence or inaction take place.

All of life is dynamic, ever-moving, ever changing. Who is to say that some seeds that you've completely ignored while you did whatever you wanted, is in suspended animation awaiting your return to minister to them?

Put a few corn seeds in the ground. Ignore them for a year. Two. What do you think you'd have? Nothing.

Have you been ignoring seeds after sacrificing and sowing them in the natural? How much would an ignored child prosper if you ignore them?

If you were making an Old Testament sacrifice, you stay at the sacrificial service until the **entire offering is received and consumed**. Birds, doves, grain – small things, but when sacrificing a goat, sheep, bullocks, oxen—staying until the entire offering is fully burned, consumed and turned into ashes, is a long time. Sowing takes more time than we modern humans give it. I'm certain of that. After staying the entire offering time, they would then go away *expecting* from God. Fully expecting from God.

The *spirit* Matters

The spirit of the Offering matters. The spirit in which you sow your seed(s) matters. For example, if you sowed in lust – **the lust for money**, then the *spirit of lust* is in you, and you will attract the spirit(s) that are attracted to lust, and that's not God.

Furthermore, if lust is in you, you can be easily drawn away by **another** lust.

If you sowed under any other work of the flesh, God may not be pleased, either;

He's not in it. Some things that man frequently does is abomination to God.

Looking at the list of what is an abomination to God. I was saddened by how wicked man is. But that's for God to judge. I was not particularly impressed that any sin is worse than another since sin is sin. But I was losing sleep over something the Holy Spirit wanted to tell me, so I chose to listen. Sexual sin is especially displeasing to Him because God is covenant-making and covenant-keeping. God wants to establish covenant with us. The establishing of covenant is very intimate. It is also life- giving when you accept it with God or His representative in the Earth.

Or it can be like-*taking* if you establish covenant with the wrong entity or wrong folks. Illegal sex is the enemy's counterfeit of making covenant. It mocks God. It does not create covenant. It creates soul ties.

Illegal Sex= Illegal Covenant= Soul Ties

Speaking of orphaning seeds and/or being drawn away by another lust, how many people – men and women have sown seeds and then been drawn away by another whole person, abandoning the ***first*** seed, the *second* seed? Seeds don't appreciate this at all.

Prayer for Abandoned Seeds

In the name of Jesus. Father, thank You, because if my own father or mother forsake or abandon me, you will take me up. You'll be a Father to the child that's left alone. You will love and protect me. Thank You, LORD, for being there when I was not sure, when I was lonely, hurt, feeling lost or defeated. With You, Lord I feel assured and protected.

*Thank You Lord, that no matter what I do, or don't do, You still LOVE me. Father, I don't have to **perform** to be loved; Your Love is unconditional. I don't have to buy love. I don't have to do anything to feel valued either here in the Earth, or in the Kingdom; I am accepted in the Beloved for just being me; the me you made me to be.*

For all those whose value has not been appreciated, even from the day of your birth, until now, may the Love of Christ find you and may you find the Lord.

I have and I am accepted in Him. I am accepted in the Beloved.

Lord, daily I receive Your tender mercies. Father, I receive Your lovingkindness. I receive Your Grace. I receive Your Truth; I receive Your Word and I receive Your Peace.

Thank You, Lord for perfecting all matters that concern me. Thank You, that in You I live and move and have my being. Thank You, Lord for good successes in my life, purpose in my life, joy. Bless you Lord, for loving relationships in my life.

I bind all spirits of lust and destruction which has caused this distraction in the supposed grown and/or spiritual people in my life.

Lord, restore all relationships that concern me and all relationships that I'm in if they are pleasing to You. ***Else Lord, I break up every covenant, every soul tie and I break camp****. In the name of Jesus. Amen.*

Multiple *Partners*, Multiple Altars

Whenever you have sex with anyone, you make a covenant with them. What do you do when it's a one-night stand and then another *opportunity* presents? Break covenant? Our God hates broken covenant. Let me rephrase that, Our God hates broken Godly covenant.

Let's say you've made an evil covenant, how do even you honor a covenant that's supposed to include only two people until the end of the Earth when you've made five, 10, 25 of them in your lifetime, through sex? And how many demons are in those 5, 10, 25 or more *counterfeit* covenants? I'm asking, how many soul ties, how many fragments of your soul are out there somewhere in the universe?

In order to have a one-night stand or any illegal sex, or a whole "relationship" with illegal sex, you and the other person either had to disregard (ignore) God, or already be serving Satan. If you weren't serving the devil before, for that 5 minutes, 10 minutes, 20 minutes, hour, night, day, or weekend—you were serving that devil. You did serve the devil. Now, you've sown seeds in the kingdom of darkness. Are you going to keep doing that thing you had so much "fun" doing and minister to that demon seed and possibly sow some more? Are you going to keep on until it harvests a crop that you'll be **ashamed** of?

They will sow wheat but reap thorns; they will wear themselves out but gain nothing. They will bear the shame of their harvest

because of the LORD's fierce anger."
Jeremiah 12:13

Or are you going to stop 🛑 and repent, hopefully never returning to your vomit? Are you going to go back to the fields of the LORD and look at the damage, devastation, and destruction you've caused to *seeds* that you have in the ground, or seedlings that were trying to thrive in the Fields of the Lord?

Hey, I'm asking for you, not for me.

Or have you just orphaned your offerings by *detaching* from them so you could go *play*? Have you just sent your offering out by itself with no tending, no parenting? Have you sent your seed out? Where? There--, while you relax and amuse yourself. Nobody told you that you had to DO something regarding your seed after you sowed it. I know. Nobody told me either. Looks like we are in this together. Thank God, for Wisdom, She's teaching us now.

If part of yourself is at the movies, fights, or beach, or in some illicit relationship not having given God a thought, no wonder your seeds are not prospering. You can't use God like a money duplicator, throwing Him a few dollars here and there while you go do what you want, asking God to multiply your money for you.

That could be why your sowing is not working. No wonder you're still not receiving 30, 60, or 100-fold. Really, if you received 30, 60 or 100-fold on even ONE offering sown, you'd be pretty comfortable.

Are you distracted? Even your **best life** can distract you. Distraction is devil trick #1, and it will not parent, minister to, or foster a 30, 60 or 100-fold return in offerings.

If you choose to break covenant or break and ungodly relationship, do you know *how* to break a covenant, to be properly free from it so in the future you can make a lasting, Godly one? I know. Nobody ever told me that either. We'll get there; keep reading.

When you just stop calling the person you most recently had sex with and ignore their texts that's not how you do it. You still have a covenant, whether you are talking to them or not, whether you are seeing them, or not.

How many other *agreements* have you made with how many other folks that you haven't kept? And with how many other folks have you been *forced* to keep, such as in business?

Been in court before a judge lately—for breaching contracts? It's all related.

Broken Hearts

So, that latest relationship *contract* you've made, is it really a covenant or is it just a soul tie? You must break soul ties. Sometimes soul ties are hard to break if one or both parties insist on hanging on. That's why folks are moping and wandering around with broken hearts by the millions. That's what's wrong with a lot of people. Even in the Body, they are brokenhearted.

That's what the afternoon talk shows are all about. Broken hearts and soul ties, and no one knows what to really call it or what to do about it. Well, God does, and Wisdom knows that God does.

Thankfully, God has provided a special anointing to heal a broken heart, (Isaiah 61:1). People are so important to God, and He loves us so much that He provides a special anointing for hurting hearts. And because He knew how tough it would be to get over a broken heart that He provided a power for this needed healing.

Maybe another reason GOD hates broken covenants is that broken hearts are almost always the fallout from a broken "covenant." God loves us and when you love someone you do not want them to hurt, if at all possible. Here's God, like a good Father, ***"I told you not to do that and now look at yourself, all hurt – let Me help you. Let Me heal you."***

My God of Mercy!

Broken hearts can be debilitating. How many brokenhearted people do you know who are properly ministering to their own *natural* seeds? Their children? Not to mention their financial, spiritual seeds? None.

Broken Hearts, soul ties and illegal covenants is a huge business. It's *distraction* and the devil is the chief executive officer, owner, and operator. How many brokenhearted people do you know who are serving God with their **whole** hearts, their whole soul? None. Healing must come first. Soul ties and devil distractions are very unprofitable to sown seeds because you need your whole soul to serve God and parent your seed, but instead because of illegal sex covenants and soul ties, your mind might be on what Johnny is doing, or where he is, or fantasizing about pornography. All the while the lust demon, a *spirit of lust* has caused a person to abandon and orphan, their seed, among other ungodly things.

You need your whole heart to serve God. You need your whole heart to minister to your children. What will become of your children if you're out in the streets looking for the next relationship? What becomes of them if you have broken up with **Mr. Right-Now** because you thought he was *Mr. Right,* and there you are, languishing in your room for the past 5 years grieving the breakup? What? Really, what? What are you thinking?

Now if there is really a physical ailment, why you might be homebound or bedridden, I am sorry and we will pray for healing of both physical and emotional/mental maladies, so your kids and seeds and relationship with God will prosper. 100. Right? 100.

You need your whole heart to minister to your spiritual seeds that you've sown for in the Offerings.

We are going to pray to break soul ties but know that every soul tie is not with another *person*. A soul can be tied to a memory, a song, a time, a place, a food – anything you keep yearning for and can't seem to break free of. Any thing that makes you *"feel some kind of way"* when you hear it or experience it and it drags you right back into a dark place. That is also a soul tie. Think on that.

Now, pray out loud…

Prayer: Breaking Soul Ties

Father, thank You for being the Lord of my life. Father, I have made ungodly soul ties, some in ignorance, some in clinginess and some are actually unknown to me. Some were interpersonal or romantic in nature and others may be familial or over close friends or things that I may admire too much—Lord, You know.

Father, God, show me all the people that I have soul ties with, show me where the fragments of my soul are, in the Name of Jesus. Father, I renounce my behavior that led to the soul ties, I break all evil, ungodly covenants by the Blood of Jesus. Lord, please forgive me for any of the ways that I opened the door for ungodly soul ties to be formed with _____ (name the person).

Father, show me all unconfessed sins with this person, or anyone else, so that I can confess them in the Name of Jesus.

*I forgive him/her and release them to live their life, prayerfully in Christ Jesus. I want to be free and **whole** to serve You, Lord, to live my life for You and free of all emotional or other pain of this soul tie.*

By the Grace of God and the Power of Your Christ, I forgive him/her in the Name of Jesus. Forgive me for the sin of entangling myself with _____ in an ungodly way. Lord, I confess all ungodly ties as sin and ask that you forgive me and cleanse me of all unrighteousness. In the power and authority of Jesus Christ, I break the ungodly soul tie between me and _____. I surrender my heart, soul, and spirit completely to Jesus Christ and His authority in my life.

*Heal me Lord, heal my heart of the effects this soul tie. Restore my soul, my will, and my intellect **(what was I thinking?)** Restore* *my* emotions. Make me whole and restore everything that the enemy stole from me.

Thank You, Lord, I am free to love You with my whole heart and love others with a Christ-like love. Thank You, Lord for making me free, ready, and available for my Kingdom spouse. In Jesus' Name, Amen.

About the Author

Dr. Marlene Miles has served in Ministry for 20+ years. She holds two Doctorate degrees in Ministry and is a dentist by day. Her joy is to share what God gives her.

Enjoy her messages on the Dr. Miles YouTube Channel, and prayers on Warfare Prayer Channel.

Books by this author

AK: Adventures of the Agape Kid

AMONG SOME THIEVES

Ancestral Powers

As My Soul Prospers

Behave

Churchzilla (Wanna-Be Bride of Christ)

The Coco-So-So Correct Show

Demonic Cobwebs

Demonic Time Bombs

Demons Hate Questions

Do Not Orphan Your Seed

Do Not Work for Money

Don't Refuse Me Lord

Every Evil Bird

Evil Touch

The FAT Demons

Fruit of the Womb: Prayers Against Barrenness, *Book 2*

got Money?

Let Me Have a Dollar's Worth

Living for the NOW of God

Lord, Help My Debt

Lose My Location

Made Perfect In Love

The Man Safari *(I'm Just Looking)*

Marriage Ed., *Rules of Engagement & Marriage*

Motherboard: *Key to Soul Prosperity*

My Life As A Slave

Name Your Seed

Plantation Souls

The Poor Attitudes of Money

Power Money: Nine Times the Tithe

The Power of Wealth

Prayers Against Barrenness, For Success in Business and Life, *Book 1*

Seasons of Grief

Seasons of War

Second Marriage, Third Marriage any Marriage

SOULS in Captivity

Soul Prosperity: Your Health & Your Wealth

The *spirit* of Poverty

This Is *NOT* That: How to Keep Demons from Coming at You

The Throne of Grace, *Courtroom Prayers*

Warfare Prayer Against Poverty

When the Devourer is Rebuked
The Wilderness Romance

Other Journals & Devotionals by this author:
The Cool of the Day – Journal
got HEALING? Verses for Life
got HOPE? Verses for Life
got WISDOM? Verses for Life
got GRACE? Verses for Life
got JOY? Verses for Life
got LOVE? Verses for Life
He Hears Us, Prayer Journal
I Have A Star, Dream Journal
I Have A Star, Guided Prayer Journal,
J'ai une Etoile, Journal des Reves
Let Her Dream, Dream Journal *in colors*
Men Shall Dream, Dream Journal,
My Favorite Prayers (in 4 styles)
My Sowing Journal
Tengo una Estrella, Diario de Sueños

Illustrated children's books by Dr. Miles

Big Dog (8-book series)

Do Not Say That to Me

Every Apple

Fluff the Clouds

I Love You All Over the World

Imma Dance

The Jump Rope

Kiss the Sun

The Masked Man

Not During a Pandemic

Push the Wind

Tangled Taffy

What If?

Wiggle, Wiggle; Giggle, Giggle

Worry About Yourself

You Did Not Say Goodbye to Me

www.ingramcontent.com/pod-product-compliance
Lightning Source LLC
Chambersburg PA
CBHW070858050426
42453CB00012B/2258